Matrix of Life

L.B.STEPHENS

outskirts
press

Outskirts Press, Inc.
http://www.outskirtspress.com

ISBN: 978-1-9772-2195-7

Outskirts Press and the "OP" logo are trademarks belonging to Outskirts Press, Inc.

PRINTED IN THE UNITED STATES OF AMERICA

This book is dedicated to Roger who is constantly encouraging and to Greg and Jeanine who give me reason to succeed.

Contents

Introduction

Creating a name for my book has been the hardest part. Matrix describes this collection of poetry as well as anything. I write about many things but they can be gathered into groups, though the groups have little to do with one another. All in all, however, they are the impressions of my life.

I try and tell a story with my poems. Sometimes they are of modern life and sometimes they are based on memory. Hopefully you will find one that speaks to you.

The Childhood Years

STARS

When I was five we were at war,
and blackouts shut out city lights
but lit the flares of Heavens fires,
so bright it was not dark at all.
I don't see stars anymore
of millions that I saw when young,
I thought that I could
pull them down
if ever I was tall enough.
But now the city lights conceal,
reflecting off the urban haze
and pink night sky.
I cannot see
the glowing jewels of darkest night.

TEN YEAR OLD'S LAMENT

It is rainy and windy
creating a chill,
as I slog
through the woods
on my way
up the hill.
My mother will scold
as I come through
the door
"Don't you dare muddy
This freshly washed floor…"
"I just finished
scrubbing…" but I
won't hear more.
I can't go in
to the warm
and the dry
I'll have to
Stay outside.
I'm ready to cry.
I know! I'll go to Janet's!
Maybe her mom will bake
her great oatmeal cookies
or even a cake!
Oh no, they're not at home.
so I guess I'll go
over to see
my girlfriend Jo!
But Jo's mom doesn't bake cookies.

First Marriage

DIRECTION

It seems our ship
rides rough right now
and yet it's our ship.

It doesn't mean
it's lost or sunk.
We will complete the trip.

Sometimes we can't
quite see it seems
just what exactly
the other means

But if we ride
the storm 'til through,
we'll find just what
we each can do.

And as you know
when the winds cease
the way will clear
and we'll find peace.

Let's keep our ship
on steady course
although the way is wild
until, in a safe harbor
we can be reconciled.

War

SHILOH

Peach petals fell like snow
upon the living and the dead.
Soft scent of blossoms floating
On the water, bleeding red
from wounded men
dying, parched,
drinking from the crimson stream.
A place of peace no longer,
shattered by a mortal scream.

WAR'S RESULT

Now the hawks cry out
"Our way is right"
The man is in retreat
He fears our might."
But doves mourn broken lives,
civilian dead
and listen to the joy
with measured dread.
Prisoners kiss the hands
of soldiers, when,
as captives they can see
The shelling end.
Into the city streets
the victors go
to find devastation
grief and sorrow.
Survivors without food,
services gone,
they roam the ravaged streets,
rejected pawns.

RETURN

Returning from the war,
it seemed that he was whole
but deeply hidden scars
still took their heavy toll.
If he could only sleep,
without the horror scenes,
reliving daily fears
or punctured by his screams.
PTSD it's called
and with it daily life
is constantly upset
and living is just strife.

The Chris Poems

BEGINNING

When you say "I love you"
You do not put out strings
To ensnare me.
You offer me your love
Without entrapment
The freedom of your caring
allows me to be free
I hope that I can offer
affection without bonds,
as you have given me.

NIGHTS

The trees would whisper his name
And moonlight touch his face at night
And lit my heart as I would watch
And feel his closeness still beside me
And I would turn and settle down
With whiffs of wood smoke all around
And garden scents of green and perfume.

TEN BEAUTIFUL YEARS

We never lived together
I find that odd now, looking back,
Great heights, great depths remembered,
Tranquility now fills the lack.
We lived in love and passion,
parted with sorrow and with need.
We spent our time as partners,
But grew alone, still, friends indeed.
He turned and found another
and beckoned, laughing, in the hall.
I went on alone
Serenity my call.

THE DANCE

The band played "Lady in Red"
As he pulled me onto the floor
We danced with his arms around me
As we'd danced many times before.
Then suddenly, everything clicked
and we danced all alone on the floor.
We danced 'til the music ended.
The applause was a thunderous roar.

CHANGE

I wouldn't say we had it all
And yet we did, in our own way.
There wasn't money but we had
A paradise, a place to play
And love and laugh and share our lives
With moonlit nights and fragrant days.
A little cabin in the woods
With lovely gardens all around
And ringed with trees and bamboo fence,
Close to a lake, where frogs resound
Their mating calls, made our small world
A haven and a hallowed ground.
The clouds of life forewarned the storms
Whose fury pulled our lives apart.
We went our ways,
The cabin changed,
Became a house, but lost its' heart.
So now it stands, another's home
life circle has returned to start.

LATER

We went our ways but still a friend
Our bond of love will never end.
He helped us love gave gentleness,
encouragement and nothing less.
We all loved him,
I hope he knew.
He touched each one.
The children grew.
He's gone from us and feels no pain.
Remembered times and love remain.

THE RIVER

One day long ago
You stood beside me
As the river flowed
We watched the current
And played in the sun.
I still remember
The laughter and fun.
The green hills,
the laughter,
even the river
are all changed now,
and you are gone.

Interlude

BUDDY

My warrior friend has visited me.
Proud, wild, sensual, he moves with grace.
I offer caring sans entrapment.
No strings ensnare him. His handsome face
tells me stories of his other life
Of power. With me he shares a while,
some laughs, camaraderie, affection, a hug,
then exits with a smile.

RAVEN

Raven, flying black as night
Hidden deep within
All your power, all your might
Concealing where you've been.

Can your trickster side unfold,
Tell us what you see?
Will you, in lofty firs, grow old
And will your soul be free?

Find your center, put roots deep,
Cherish what you see.
All you have you now can keep
And in loves arms be free.

FOREST WALK

Tall trees
Dark green
Chartreuse
Subdued wonder.

First scent
then sound
then mist
and low thunder.

Brightly
splashing
tumbling,
veiled Bridal Falls

Hushed,
Awed
we hold hands
in forest halls

Travel

ON THE ROAD

I had a Volkswagen Eurovan
And with it I was free
To see this glorious land of ours
from mountains to the sea.

To feel the awesome power
Of Niagara's roar
To gaze into Grand Canyon
and watch the condors soar.

I drove the Mother Road,
Sixty-six by name
And saw the rippling prairie
That Steinbeck brought to fame.

I camped in parks
both big and small
or boon docked
in a handy mall.

They don't make them anymore
so they are obsolete
but traveling in my Eurovan
was a special treat.

STORM WAVES ON MAUI

Small droplets
of the sea
fell softly
on my skin
while savage waves
trembled the earth.
How can such
gentleness
and power
be contained
in one small space?

HOLIDAY

We came to Hawaii for sunshine
instead we were deluged by rain.
I found out Springtime is rainy.
I'll remember when we come again.

The call of the islands still beacons,
it is always a great time to be,
To relax seeking shells on the beach,
watching waves as you walk by the sea.

Plumeria just started blooming
Bougainvillea blooms purple and red.
The shrimp trucks still sit by the roadside
whenever you need to be fed.

I'm glad we came back to Hawaii.
we have many fond memories from here.
The music, the dance and the flowers
All add enjoyment each year.

CANYON DU CHELLY.
(Chelly is pronounced Shay)

I sat near the rim
of Canyon Du Chelly
and heard down below
a flute player play.

His magic told stories
of sun stars and moon,
then suddenly stopped.
It ended too soon.

But I will remember
'til my dying day
the sunset I heard
the flute player play.

COLUMBIA

Maryhill stands stark
atop the towering hill
and Stonehenge reproduced
is a mystery still.

Fishing boats are on the water
And some fish from the shore.
The parks are filled with families
seeking petroglyphs and more

The mighty dams hold back
The water for the farms
and produce needed electricity
But cause salmon runs harm

Windsurfers ride the currents
Their sails like bright balloons
Wildflowers bloom profusely and
waterfalls dance many tunes

HAIGHT-ASHBURY

I was a Hippie,
Do you know what I mean?
When I look back now
It all seems a dream.

To smell the patchouli
as you walk in the Height,
but never with anything
as bourgeois as a date.

To sit with your friends
For "Music in the Park"
Passing a doobie,
Alert for a narc

Music was everywhere
Morning night and day.
The Airplane landed
But the Starship flew away.

The "Summer of Love"
and yes, it was free,
communes and protests,
and new things to see.

So much that was novel,
new experiences, too
new ideas shared
by a mystic guru.

Bell bottoms, head bands,
men with long hair
it all was magic.
You had to be there.

Life Today

FREEWAY

You can't get there from here,
no matter where you go.
Driving on the "Freeway"
the only speed is slow.
The driver just in front of me
can't merge with other cars.
He stops and starts
And starts and stops,
makes this lane move like tar.
Now comes the racing driver
as in and out he swerves,
going too fast for safety
as he heads into the curves.
OH! Now the whole freeway's closed,
A truck has lost his load.
We will have to detour
on a muddy, bumpy road.
There is an HOV lane,
but you have to pay to use.
Traveling on the "freeway"
is nothin' but the blues.

WAITING

I'm waiting still on hold
to complete my call,
listening to music
I don't like at all.
Now that is I interrupted
by voices that say
that they "appreciate my call,"
then answer it today,
I guess I'll have to wait
to complete my task.
. Answering the blinking phone
is not too much to ask.

RAIN

Although I love
the sound of the rain,
getting out in it
I still disdain.
I don't like cold water
dripped down my neck
or cold wet feet.
Oh, what the heck!
Rain brings the beauty
the green and the lush.
The glorious beauty
is worth the rush.
I'll wait for the sun
And cheer when it shines.
I'll play and get warm,
And have some great times!

BUILDING MY GARDEN

"I'm going to play in the garden"
is what I like to say,
and that is where you'll find me,
almost any sunny day.
I started with a weed patch,
two tons were tossed away,
and then it needed terraces
and flowers for each day.

A tiny stream runs through it
at the bottom of the hill,
and even in the summertime
it is never still.

But it is more than work and plants,
a place of contemplation.
A place to study and to think
and satisfy frustration.

Whenever I am angry
and want to scream and shout,
I grab another weed, yell" die"
and yank it out.

So come and visit some fine day
I'd like for you to see.
I won't even make you work
But just enjoy with me

DON'T MESS WITH MAMA

I watched today
a full act of a play
as a crow tried to take
a wren's nest away.
It was fiercely defended
by the tiny mother
and she was soon joined
by her clan of brothers.
A whole act written
of a destroyer chased away
by a clan of tiny birds
who really saved the day.

FISH ON!

"Fish on" I called, excited
feeling the tugging line,
another perfect fishing day
and the weather's fine.

"This one is big" I thought
it can't be just wall-eye.
Oh wow! It is a sturgeon
and it's as big as I.

I battled and I fought it,
it tugged and jumped and ran.
The sun was hot. I played the fish
as well as any can.

Then it is beside the boat
and now five feet are measured!
The fish is out of season, damn!
I must release my treasure

So we're back to wall-eye
and we catch a mighty bunch.
We congratulate ourselves
as we dock and eat our lunch.

It's great as we remember
the perfect fishing day.
Warm time upon the river,
a time of fun and play.

The Joys of Growing Old

BIRTHDAY CHILD

My son is 52 today
but how CAN that be?
for I am only 65
or so it seems to me.
I know that in reality
he really is that old
and I am hardly 65
if the truth be told.

It's strange, as I grow older
my years don't fit my age.
I'm always so much younger
in my mind or on the page,

And yet I'm proud of living
to seventy or more.
I've seen so many changes
from times that came before.
.I really hope to reach my goal
to live one hundred three
because one hundred is so trite
and that is not for me

For I am somewhat quirky
some say "pleasantly unique",
I need to go my own way
and I am hardly meek.

So I try to celebrate,
this job of growing older,
I really work to live each day
as my world grows colder.
"Growing old is not for sissies"
Like Bettie Davis stated,
but I feel that I've been lucky
for me to be so fated.

REMEMBER?

Where on earth is my coffee cup?
Oh! It's in the refrigerator
It should be in the microwave.
I'll get the cream out later.

I go into another room
Where I think I've left my book.
If I remember when I get there
I'll really have to look

I hope that I can find it soon
Before I have forgotten
just who the noble hero is
and who is really rotten

Oh! Where did I leave my slippers?
Are they underneath the bed?
Or can they be found
in the laundry room instead.

I hope it doesn't get much worse.
It really is one of my fears.
I'd love to blame it on old age,
But it's been going on for years.

WINNING

They played Cribbage every night
She'd won three weeks in a row.
It was just a lucky streak.
His streak was a month ago.

They were well matched
Alternating who won
And no one could see
who the winner would be
until the game was done.

She laughed as he
sat down to play.
He said that maybe
this will be his day.

"It's not too likely"
she did say,
but he won! The last laugh
was his today,

DONA SEBASTIANA

Dona Sebastiana is the Queen of the Dead in the
Mexican culture and is always displayed on La Dia
Del Morte dressed beautifully. In my mind's eye she
is a caring young and beautiful woman who will hold
my hand softly as I pass across that last bridge. It is
quite comforting.

Dona Sebastiana
Is waiting for me I know,
but even if she comes to call,
I don't believe I'll go.
For life is too exciting,
so much to learn and play,
I'll tell her come back later,
I'm much too busy today.

Biography

I was born in the Pacific Northwest and except for various times in Idaho, Oregon, California Nebraska, Illinois and Georgia totaling about 15 years. I have always returned to the beauty of the Pacific Northwest. I have loved the weather, rainy as it might be as it provides perfect gardening weather and secures the lush greenery that surrounds us. As they say here, I have webs between my toes. I am surrounded by water and mountains and lush green forests.

I have been proud of my ancestry ever since I discovered that the women in my family have been able to read and write since early centuries even at times when only small percentages of the population were able to do so. I am also the product of five centuries of newspaper editors and publishers, but the ancestors I relish the most are Desire Howland and Temperance Gorham who have been in the United States from its founding. I believe their names fit me, in both meanings of the word, and I am a daughter of Temperance, a daughter of Desire. I am a curious person, for which I am most grateful for that generous gift from God.

Poetry is my latest creative outlet for I have done much more in earlier years: painting, dance, design. Again I am most grateful to the generosity of God for gifting me with this wonderful way of expressing my world

CPSIA information can be obtained
at www.ICGtesting.com
Printed in the USA
LVHW021300150520
655581LV00004B/595